Surprise Me

Grace Murphy

For my late grandmother, Ann Moss, also known as Ghee. You're still everything to me. For my husband, Matthew & our dog, Beckett - loves of my life. For my mom, & inspiration Michelle, my incredibly kind & brilliant dad, Eric, my radiant little sister, Hayley, and my future brother-in-law, Sam. For my cousin, Jake, thank you for believing in me, it has changed my life. For Sophia, Lad, and Dana. For Adam, Julia, Asa, and Elio. For my Aunt Pattie & Uncle Mark, thank you for your support. For my Grandpa Art, & Grandma & Grandpa Murphy. Thank you for your lessons. For my in-laws, Linda & George Evanoff, who let me use their backyard as an office while I wrote this book. For Mark, Rebecca, Hannah, Hayden, Payton, and Roman. I love all of you so much.

For every single person that battles depression, and anxiety.

For every student I've ever had the privilege to teach, and finally for O'Reilly's, the pub that raised me.

ACT I

MAGIC

They tell me you
suffer from spells
often but do they
know you hold
all the magic?

EXPOSE

You come broken,
and try to hide what's
already known. But I
expose your scars to
the heavens and paint
them in gold, so you
can witness how
stunning you are,
as you are.

SO EASY

It is so easy to mean
what you say. Just
shatter your heart
open, and give up
everything you
thought you knew.

Throw away things
that just don't taste
right anymore.

Move on from what
once cemented you
in place, unable to
explore what's already
at your fingertips.

The feelings you hold
inside could make
the sea overflow.

STUNNING

I borrow the moon
so you can see yourself
in her reflection.
You are so beautiful.

So stunning in your
stride. So stunning
in your laugh.

You're a child
of the sun. The
light & you
were made
for each other.

BORROW

You are an angel in your
own LA dimension of
determination and auras.

Your heart breaks, but
it doesn't quit. You find
warmth in the wreckage,
and turn debris into destiny

Ask the LA sunrise if
you can borrow her colors.
Maybe she can fill the
fractures of your soul
with a fresh start.

LED

She had adventure
in her blood, trouble
in her bones, and a
led foot for the open
road. There was no
stopping her.

READ

I read the transcript
sent from the moon.

She sent the letter
through the stars,
the mountains,
the rivers, the lakes,
the ocean, the lions,
the dogs, & the salamanders.

Just to say: Keep going.

BET

Someone prepared you a
cocktail of your insecurities,
and you drank that bait
like a drunk swallows
champagne from a bottle.

You were easy to break.
And she knew it.
That kernel of truth
you got wasted on.

She made a bet you'd
choke on it, before asking
for help, and won big.

IF I

If I arrive with sun
shining in my head,
and I leave you
with a cloud in
my heart. I can't
come back to that.

SHOW YOU

I don't have the
map for an easy time,
but I can show you
how to chisel away
at boulders until you
find a source of light.

You don't need
to explain the
way your light moves,
how it changes in the
fall of a petal, and
rests like rain on
your vision.

INVITES

The desert wind calls
her name, invites her
to wander. Encourages
her to get lost, so she
can see herself in the sand.

You find her at the
crossroads of a snake,
and a fox, but she finds
magic where people claim
there is none.

She's lost to you now.
You try to forget with
whisky but each time
the bottle hits your lips,
you undress another
memory, and drown in desire.

DON'T

Don't get to the point.
Take the long way.
Show me where
you buried your secrets.

We can run through
orchards & I can play
with your curls.

We can question everything
we see. Turn over every
long exhale until we find
the right words.

SIP

I sip on my coffee,
and slip on a layer
of faith for the day.

There are always
monsters on my trail,
but we've become
generous together,
sometimes they even
tell me where to go next.

NEEDED

You needed magic
to intervene that night,
you needed the stars
on your side, and the
universe to bend to
the sound of your
heart beat.

But magic doesn't
Just appear when
you say so. It's a
practice. You have to
show up everyday.
Forever.

DIDN'T KNOW

I didn't know I could
do this. Didn't know
if I could put myself
on this line.

Why not? He asked.
It's your only war.

ADVENTURE

I need an adventure
like a bird needs its song.
Like roots need water.

Like trees need space
Like writers need rain.
Like lovers need Paris
Like LA needs sunshine
Like the world needs you.

HIDDEN

She took everything
hidden & turned
it to light.

WEAVE

You weave the Siren's
name in lightning
without knowing.

Your screams
bounce off seashells.
& poke the siren in the side.

Meanwhile, you bury
all that's delicate.
She arrives and helps
you find what you
think you've lost.

Why would you even
think about throwing away
something so beautiful?

CHASE

You wanted to chase
something never-ending,
and you wanted to find
people who understood that.

Now you ride with winds
so fast, you're impossible
to measure.

You tap into the stars,
into me. like its nothing,
you are practiced & patient.

I've seen you move
the earth from its axis
when inspired.

GIVE

I give your heavy heart
all the light I can find.
I want you to know
yourself again.

We go through
old photos, And
I see. It's always
been there.

I though that
sparkle only
existed in the movies.

I give your soul
all the music I know.
I want to shake you
from your slump.

Reverse the curses
of your past thoughts,
so you can hear
your song again.

FRENCHMAN

You asked to know
her pried open steel
rode down her river
on a bed of rocks.

Took her to a Frenchman
in Louisville who
confirmed the song
in her heart.

CAN'T

We can't go back to
the way things were,
and I don't want to.

Truth is damning like that.

TO D.

*They don't understand
the miracle,* my friend said.
Funny, I replied. *I always
thought they didn't
understand the death.*

We meet people
In the middle
all the time .

It's hard to get it
when you've never
had it.

STOPPED

You've stopped letting
love in. People have to
trespass across cavernous
stretches of privacy to see
a glimpse. And why?

What are you hiding?
What is so horrible
about the truth of
you?

MOST

What surprised me
about grief?

It's the beautiful
moments where
I miss you most

It seems unfair how
every part of you
freezes & life
still moves on.

For many years, I
have used this river
of grief to water wilting
flowers, and you'd be
surprised how many times
they rise again.

TOLD YOU

I told you, I had a thing
for trouble, You tried
to kiss me.

But I couldn't stay.
didn't want to have you.
& leave you.

Miss a man I never
knew like this just
ain't right.

LOST

I hold on to your every
word, because I see how
lost they are on everyone else.

CLOSER

She can hold you
captive in her magic,
& release your burdens
in the same breath .

This man right here
was drunk on her
magic, and all
the better for it.

But the loss, oh
the loss. The empty
bottles & emptier thoughts.

Somebody come get him
he's at it again. Hating
himself is his religion.

GO FISH

You were hoping
to destroy me, but
I created a heaven
from your hell.

& every time you
made me feel unsafe,
I became more dangerous.

Go fish.

HISTORY

We find ways to heal
from the history
left on these
shores.

Some of us say
nothing to each
other.

Seperated by values
by old fueds. By unsaid
love, and things we don't
even know. Or never did.

We say we'll stop it.
Will we? We say
we'll be better this
time. Different?

MAD-MAN

It takes a mad-man
at peace with himself
to love a woman in
constant battle with
her angels.

A woman who
messes with gravity.

It takes a kind man
who knows the war
to love a woman
who misses it.

A woman who
simmers from
the bottom of
the ocean floor.

.

HUMAN

There's something
supernatural about
how human you are.

You run hot, stew
in baths of bitterness.
I ask if you need
chocolate.
You do.

When you do allow
touch, it has to
start so slow.

NEVER

It's dawn at Stinson beach.
I'm just wondering, he said.
When you're gonna let
yourself off this
hook?

He never tried
to understand
all my phases
I can't explain,
& don't want to.

GONE

When her name
was mentioned,
he left to sip his
whisky in the rain fall.

Did as he always does
when he can't stay
fake.

Brooded in empty alleys,
chain smoked, and hit
his head against a
million memories.

.

ACT II

I MET A GENIUS TOO, BUKOWSKI

I heard a genius
on the train yesterday.
About 5 years old,
she stood beside me
& as the train Swayed
back-and-forth along
tracks We came to the stop.
& then she held onto me & said,
Monsters are ridiculous
It was what I needed to know.

WAIT

My breath is caught
In your words
your looks
your lies.

DIAMOND

You think faster
than anyone I know.
Something about
your mind in this
light, makes me
want to know you.

You invent languages
few can hear. Is it lonely?
Do you yearn for Moscow?
And what's it like
to hold the moon?

ANGELS

If you listen to the chorus
of angels, you'll find the
trail to your heart, with
all the music notes
they left behind.

DAUGHTER

I am the poet's daughter.
She creates symphonies
from ash. I always
knew the stars favored her.

When God saw her
unknown trail he gifted
her with secrets only
the planets know so
she could survive, and
she did. & I am just
lucky to stand in her light.

STRUCK

They were struck
by your ability
to catch lightning
in your lips.

You loved them for
all the the words
they left on their tongue.

All the looks you
gave them when people
spoke for too long
of nothing.

RICH DADS

You learn to listen
to the ocean from
the valley. You see
princesses everywhere,
on to their next party
where rich dads make
sadder passes.

BE

My heart is
in orbit.
Leave her be.

TILL I DON'T

I have all the room
in the world until
I don't. Patience like
nature until there's none left.

I'll open my door,
set you up with warmth,
and even let you stay a while.

But if you ever forget,
even for a moment,
that I can be your
coldest winter night,
and place nothing, but
icebergs between us,
I'll remind you.

IF I LOVE

If I love you,
and if you'll let me,
I'll hike to the highest
peak of your history,
and learn to love you better.

SO LOUD

The night she met him,
her heart sang so loud,
it was hard to sleep.
And even now I only
sleep to dream of you.

BUKOWSKI

In my apartment
in East Hollywood:
on the same block
where Bukowski lived
in the sixties.

In my complex I take
my dog out to pee,
but he doesn't have to
pee.

He's a liar, he just
likes his face in the
sun. And it reminds
me. I like my face in
the sun as well.

It's a light wind
on a sixty-three
degree day in the
dead of winter.

It reminds
me of San Francisco.
A trumpet plays
from two doors down.

BE HUNGRY

It's not enough
to be good.

You have to
be hungry.

It has to mean
more than yourself.

REMIND

You remind me of
a place I've never
been to, but know
in my bones.

A WHILE

If love sounds clumsy
coming out of my
mouth, Forgive me.
It's been a while since
I've let someone see me real.

Since I've let someone
hold me without holding
my breath. Since I've let
someone love me on purpose.

SELFIE

You send a selfie
as you're about to walk
down the aisle, Give an
oath to a man you don't know.
For what?

In December you stole
Johnny Cash's guitar,
a spanking new Cadillac,
and made love with a batch of lies.

You are haunted in this picture,
a cliché of yourself.
I tip-toe my response.

Your veil with glued
on sparkles makes
me spin in grief.

You have forgotten
the space between
yourself and the sky.

And he will keep you
in The Doll House
until a gunshot is heard.

FORTUNE

Choose another fortune,
one that fits your laugh.
Look how the light
slants in your presence.
That office sipped out
my soul, and spit
it in quicksand.

To survive, I parked
my heart in neutral.
Promised myself
it wasn't forever.
That panic attack.
I crawled off the
red line like a drunk baby.

Visions of cartoon stars
circling above me.
I stopped pretending
like this life wasn't
going to kill me and left.
I heard another trail wanting.

PORTAL

A portal opened, and
I dove. Perfect Ten.
Just kidding. I broke
my head open, because I
didn't even look before
I left land.

Furious storms revealed
what is underneath the
floorboards. After I
saw what I saw,

I had to put my
brain back together
like Jenga, and it
took more than
a minute

Any wrong move,
and the whole structure
collapsed. God saying,
try again.

NO CHOICE

I chase the north star,
outrun fallen angels,
and take leaps of faith
so big the mountains
have no choice but to move.

WAIT

I wait till the sun
goes down, and invite
night into my room.

The stars rock me to sleep.
I dream of any galaxy
where I can find you.

UNVEIL

You unveil the storm
in your soul like
it might scare me.

Like you're the
first madman
I've weathered.

The first genius
to uproot my world.

Even the lone wolf
needs a somebody.

SOMETIMES

Sometimes your words
float in my head like
tiny clouds hanging
over my thoughts.

Your words hail
hard, without
mercy, just the
Devil.

Your words catch
my sight, hurt
what's already
infected.

WITNESS

If I wanted, I could
wrap you in sunlight,
and point out exactly
where you sparkle.

For some people,
it will hurt at first.
And there is no turning back.

I could be witness
to all your mistakes.
I could ask the mountains
to forgive the worst
thing you've ever done,
and if they whisper,
My God, kid. Haven't you suffered enough?

Then maybe you've suffered enough.

NOTHING

It's like I'm full,
and empty at the
same time. Nothing
excites me There are
blinks of relief,
and then it's
there again.
That monter.

I am tired of slicing
myself into pieces just
to fit such boring puzzles.
It's getting too hard to
hide all the galaxies
in my heart.

TOO HARD

It was too hard
for you to see me
happy, so you kicked
me wayside, because
you only like me when
I'm down and out.

My light turned on
offends you, and
if that isn't the
biggest turn off.

UNWILLING

There's a fire in my
soul I'm unwilling
to put out. And I can't,
anyway.

If you come with with
war on your hands, I will
not disappoint you.

Please don't tap
my glass.

EVERYBODY

Your heart is a one of a kind
wild that comes with a
song everybody knows.

AROUND YOU

I take deep breaths
think before I speak
put smiley faces
in my emails, and
apologize for nothing.
Not for nothing.

I apologize for something
worse than nothing. I
apologize for being right.
Almost every time, because
you don't like the way
my ideas sound not
coming out of your mouth.

You want my knowledge.
You want my money.
My time, my energy
my effort, but you
can't handle me. And
you think my time,
my energy, my effort
is somehow disconnected
from me.

You think you can
have one without the other,

and that is why you
don't know what it's
like to put in my time,
my energy my effort.

Your lazy brains are
an antidote to anything great.

You stole the music
but you'll never play
my song.

SORRY

I could drown in
your sorry's. Every other
word is a sorry. It means
nothing. Pebbles.

I swallow the lies
on your lips,
brainwash myself
to feel better.

BE HONEST

Be honest with me
and strip your words
to kisses.

You think you know
better than that.
But you don't know
me yet.

Maybe you don't know
anything. It's more
fun that way.

THOUGHT

I think you thought
we had time. But
I always knew there
would never be enough of it.

EXHALE

That loud exhale tells
me all the things
you're trying not to say.

But this full moon
was made for us.
Crafted for our cries,
and lit with desperation.

LIGHTNING

You can't catch the wind,
and you can't catch her.
Just because you capture
lightning in a bottle doesn't
mean you know the eye of the storm.

COWBOY

He sat on the table,
put his foot on the chair.
Cowboy boots, he told me,
Say a lot about a man.

I pulled up my skirt
and showed him mine,
covered in dirt & hope.

So what do these
Say about me? I asked.

Everything.

SOME DAYS

There are some days
when I'm over it all,
but I still want
everything.

Today all I can do
is watch the rain
fall & listen to you
rant over the world.

HERE

Look around. If flowers
can grow after destruction
so can we.

I smolder our future
in sage, we need some
angels on the inside.

The corners of your shadows
do not worry me. I'm
worried you've forgotten
your worth.

CALLS

Sun breaks, and
the beach calls,
your breath yields
to the ocean air,
your pulse finds
its beat in the beyond.

Even the crabs are
happy to see you.

Deep breaths of relief
as mist rests on your
forehead. Maybe today
can be better.

A THOUSAND

It took a thousand pink
sunrises, and salt water
on my lips before I
remembered how to
come home.

But I still wake up
unsatisfied, craving
adventure, so I make
plans for fresh views,
and tell my friends
I'll meet them on old
roads of a new country.

HOWEVER

Give yourself the
space to feel however
you want to feel.

You can daydream, and
mourn in the same space.
I do it all the time.

You are not born for
other people to make
sense of you.

That's between you
and your God.

UNDER

We drive as far
as faith will take us,
bury our doubts in
the sand, and let the
waves wash us home.

Trust the ocean knows
something I don't. Trust
that land is in reach.

This path of least
resistance is too
hard for me. —

I KNOW

I know where you'll find him.
He's at a broken down bar,
on the windiest corner of Chicago.

I know where you'll find him.
Slamming doors in his huge,
and hollow apartment.

I know where you'll find him.
Losing himself in white
dream dust & losing all of us
One. Slammed Door. At a time.

NEVER

You must have swallowed
your whole ego to end
up here in front of me.
Asking for my help.
After all this time.

You reach out, and
I take another step
back. You touched
me once, and I was
cold for five years.

You want to pay
for the past, but
your debts have been
forgiven here.

I would never accept
a penny for your
thoughts nevertheless
a *sorry* you could
never mean.

WALK

I take a walk
in my head, and
face all the demons
that once made me run.

Demons that once made
my head shrivel in light,
and steal my sleep.

Demons that once made
me think all the angels
had abandoned me.

THROUGH ME

There was a musicican
who saw right through
me, but there wasn't
anything romantic about it.

He was a messenger.
I would only cross
paths with once.
He told me a secret
that follows me everywhere.

Even my angels are wicked,
always raising hell
just to entertain the
heavens.

But that's not the secret.

MUSIC

Bad days aren't turned
down here. I play
the music of silence,
know all the colors
of anger by heart,
and can promise no
waterfalls of regret
will go unloved.

OFFER

All you could offer
was judgement, said you
didn't know me anymore.

So I took my trial
to the trains, and rode
across state lines until
I met strangers who
offered mercy.

Said they knew me
all too well.

LEAVE

You have to leave
things behind. People,
feelings, talismans, all of it.

They think you're alone,
but you're just a
soldier of the stars,
drawn to the calls
of desert winds.

Still learning how to
answer on time.

WALK

You ask me to
take a walk in the
storm, and accidentally
admit your love under
breaks of thunder.

One last attempt to
drown out the truth.
But I can't stand here
anymore.

I can't stand here
anymore. It kills me
to see you pretend
this is the life you
want.

UNDER

It's the witching hour
on a full moon, and
I am under your spell.

With each minute that
passes, I fall in love
with you all over again

We sit in silence among
the sequoias. We can hear
history speak. Enchanted leaves
spell out a new future.

FAITH

I forgot what faith
felt like. Lost myself
in the noise.

Saw everyone's path
except my own. Always
bracing for my life.
Jaw locked so tight
it ticks like a clock.

Shoulders to my ears.
Inescapable breath.
Permanently on.

Then I felt my chest
warm up. I freed
the grief I've held
hostage in my rib cage.

I had to jump start the dragon
in my heart, and
breathe fire back into
my life.

CREATIVES

I feel raw. Scared
to death of failing.

I take a deep breath,
take the dog for a walk,
Visit my favorite plant.

Remember the sacrifices
People made for me
to have such easy worries.

LET YOU

I let you see the
parts of me I don't
even show myself.

You see me in a light
I thought went out
a long time ago.

Who are you to
uncover me like this?
Please don't leave now.

MAKE IT

To survive in Los Angeles
is to make it.

LA is the future, and
the past at once.

A scattered city with
one giant heartbeat.

THE START

It was clear you
were different from
the start.

Your light just kept
burning and burning.
Until it dawned on me:
You are endless.

Ever-changing,
ever-evoloving,
devouring information
for every meal.

A pulse so strong it's
a little distracting.

STEALING

You're not stealing
glances, you're begging
for them. In front
of everyone.

What would I say
if I came from
a higher place?

Only if I had
to say it, would I
say: All those
memories:

I still love them.

NIGHTS

I don't miss you.
I just miss those
nights.

That time in our life.
Where decisions didn't
seem so permanent.

ORB WEAVER

You spun our love
into a cobweb so
strong it caught
everyone else in our trap.
You wanted to make
movies, and I wanted
to be your star.

But then I realized
I didn't want to be
the girl of your dreams.
I wanted to be
the woman of my own.

Spin my own web.
Write my own stories.
Make my own films,
be my own everything.

BE HERE

The lights are bright.
The cameras click &
it's still not enough.

You know she should
be here. With you.

Later that night you
undress your memories
in front of everyone
through sips of whisky.

TRIED

Every time you tried
to keep her small,
the universe expanded.

EXPERIENCE

Love isn't delicate
silk that unravels
with tears, love
is a fighter with
experience.

Maybe I'm more like
the ocean than I like
to admit. Calm one
moment, deadly
the next.

My inspiration runs fast,
and hot. Without any
notice she escapes any
package anyone tries
to ship her in.

She is a bitch who
has burned me, left
me scarred, and made
me love my life.

SWEET

It's hard for me
to be sweet as pie,
when I'm made from
lost stars and stones.

If I wanted to be polite
all the time, I wouldn't
have decided to become
an artist. You can't do both.

I won't keep everything
inside and let poison manifest
until it's released without
my consent.

Let my words shake,
just know that I won't.

HELL

You brought hell
to my doorstep, and
forced my feet to fire.
That's how I learned
I could fly.

I can look at you now:

All those edges softened
into love, like I thought
they would.

But I still remember
how it hit when
your Devil ran in
my veins.

I've never been afraid
of the caves. I just don't
want to live there.

But you,
you could never leave.

VISION

Her vision was never
better after surviving
another long walk
through the fog.

THE MIDDLE

The middle of the race
is the hardest. Doesn't
matter if you had a
good start, you could
lose it here. You could
also win it here.

Actually, you can only
win it here. Even if
another boat wins
by an inch at the
very end, that inch
was won in the middle.

When no one was looking.
No end in sight.
When everything hurt.
When you decided
you had more to give
than lose.

OF COURSE

Of course you're here
at the beach, drowning
your regrets in a bottle
of red, and confessing
sins even the ocean
can't swallow.

Begging for more attention
than the moon herself.
My God, man. Pull yourself together.

You made this sea.
Swim in it. Set sail,
and drop your anchor
somewhere you actually
like to be.

If you cross our oceans
of silence because your
roots need water, you
better come with flowers.

TAKE

Some people take
so much from you
that when you do
something for yourself,
they feel robbed.

YOU KNOW

You know you love
yourself when it's easy
to love other people too.
A kind of peace that
thickens your skin,
and softens your heart.

BETTER

You hypnotized me with
lies, and I fell under
your trance.

It was too easy for me
to belive I was bad
than to admit I
deserved better.

SONG

That old song
is traveling the globe.
Dropping notes into
the ears of artists who
can shake things
 into place.

Aristry is a practice
in prayer. It requires
tremendous faith,
not only in yourself,
but others as well.

APOLOGY

Your apology is a
dollar short and a
million lies too late.

You couldn't pick my
heart from a hole in
the ground.

Nobody wants some shallow
smoke and mirrors truce,
some soiled olive branch,
all withered from use.

BACKBONE

Have some backbone.
At least borrow some
of mine.

At the end of the night,
I need to be good
with God.

My consicence is more
important than spineless
affirmations.

PLEASE

Please arrange lilies on
my skin under a pink
supermoon, and make
a mess of me.

Show me the grit
your soul is made from.
I'll trace your history
with a lovers touch,
and we'll dance until
you remember the beat
of your own heart again.

CELEBRATE

I celebrate my ruin,
and you can't fight
the compulsion to fix me.

But I know how to swim
in the deep end, I know
the ocean floor, and
I rise when I want to.

KNOWING

I miss your knowing
nods, and the way we had
to stifle our laughter every
time we we caught
something other people
couldn't see.

I tried to ignore the
familairity between us,
pretend I didn't recognize
you from another life.

It took control I didn't
know I had to stop myself
from saying, *Hey, you and me,
we're the same.*

NO ONE

You played the guitar
like no one, and I felt
every chord the way
a siren feels every
note of the ocean.

I love a human on
all cylinders. At
full force. All at
once.

Sparks for fingers, and
a voice so rough
it made me cry.

LAYER

I sip on my coffee,
and slip on a layer
of faith for the day.

There are always
monsters on my trail,
but we've become generous
together, sometimes they
even tell me where to go next.

DIDN'T DON'T RATHER

I didn't raise hell,
hell raised me.

I don't bite my tongue,
it's too sharp.

&

I'd rather walk on fire
than pins and needles.

CENTER

I chased every single
shooting star in sight,
and found you at the
center of all my wishes.

A SMIRK

You were the one.

Standing in front
of the taxi, hat in hand,
and a smirk that made
a woman wonder.

You didn't rush your words,
just lifted your cowboy
hat instead.

*You want to be boring
or have an adventure?*

Please understand
I had no choice.

DANCE

We dance under
the desert galaxy,
and feel breath
reach our bodies again.

We float on the moon,
and dazzle on the
forecasts of our future.

We arrive late to coffee
that mornig, still dripping
in magic from the night before.

METHOD

The method to your
madness always made
sense to me.

So dawn on me.
Light me up, and
rearrange destiny.
I love a life on fire.

I LOVE

I love how she doesn't
hate herself into silence.
how she won't give up
exactly what she sees.

I love how she's often
on nobody's side
except her own.

I love how her heart
often lands in a
giant question mark.

OUR WARS

We survive our wars
in hopes for a fighting
chance with harmony.

Pray to the mountains
for a pat on the shoulder.

Dampen our hair in amethyst.
Kick our feet up on clouds,
and ask for answers
we're afraid we already know.

If the Magic 8 ball
is right, heal your
wasted brain into motion.

kiss your bones,
and apologize,
surrender the cruel
words you've kept in
a penny jar.

OLD MAN

She convinces herself
the old man in Chicago
never loved anyone.
But that's not true,
no matter what he
wants you to believe.

So when you see
the old man in Chicago
with a coyote face,
twigs for bones,
his father's black coat,
and the weight of regret,
say nothing.

He'll have a Pabst,
and a shot of Maker's.
He won't buy his
own cigarettes, but
on a drunken night
he'll accept one of yours.

GRIEF

She strips us of sunrises.
Tangles our stomachs with ivy.

Blows fog in our ears.
She shows up uninvited,
overdressed, and furious.
She's not wrong, just loud.
Unreasonable.

But she gives violins
their scent, stops people
from being crushed by
picket white fence plots.
What do you do?
Grief, the Queen of
HardknockHope,
gives women like us
scepters fused from
thrown out bottle caps.

We do backflips on tightropes,
appear in loveless deserts
filled with no's and show
you constellations of possibilities.

ENTIRE LIFE

Is this what happens
when you are misunderstood
your entire life?

I've seen you hand your heart
over to anyone who doesn't show
you judgement. But you deserve
more than decency.

You deserve the kind of love
that stops time.

FIND YOU

Did they find you rotting
in your own filth?
My heart hiccups when
I see your picture.

Just admit it. You ran down
the midnight street, because
you wanted my gown ruined
in rain that night. You wanted
to taste my words in your mouth,
and paint me in your love.

But it wasn't the stars,
destiny, or what you
called, "kismet."

You were a Devil in daylight,
and all I wanted to
do was dance.

A HINT

All it takes is a hint
of your scent in a
crowded bar, and
I suffocate.

A man suffering from a
painful psychosis on the street
breaks a glass bottle
on my foot as I pass by.

I pull out shards of blood-stained
glass like it's nothing.

I've been killed, burried,
burned before. Still can't
get the dirt out.

WITNESS

You came here because
you left yourself with
no other options.

You took off because
you did not feel whole.

& I know you lost your
compass on purpose.

Instead of tracking
the stars, you surrendered
to the wind.

She warned you:
You'll never be half
anything ever again.

NICE

I'm glad I took moments to look
at us in the same place,
at the same time,
and think

This is nice.

HAD TO

I had to let you go,
so I could hold on
to myself.

Even the heavens
couldn't fill that
void in you.

My seas part from yours
I don't have time for
the middle ground.

I don't trust
the middle ground.
It's not so steady.
I don't get how you
can cut your heart
in half at a whim
& expect people
to give you
their all.

THE LAKE

We row on the lake,
before the day wakes up,
& with every stroke
we pray on everything
we once slept on.

With every stroke
we move closer to God.
And further away from
the thoughts that
distract us from gold.

The boat moves fast
but not fast enough.
We slow down the pace
and push harder.

I onced watched a boat
win by a long mile
without ever changing
their pace. Their breath
still full by the end. I
wanted to win like that.

REMEMBER

We cross paths, and
I remember there's no
such thing as coincidence.

I've been waiting for
this moment. You deserve
the worst. So I give
you my best.

I can only pray that
Johnny is right, and
God's gonna get you.

MUSES

When you were born
the muses screamed your
name like they'd been
waiting for your arrival.

Your electric soul makes
the whole city sparkle.

& I think it bothers
them how stardust
rests in our hands.

MORE TRUTH

Hot nights in Hollywood,
too much tequila, and
even more truth.

Give me that LA summer.
I want to take you
downtown on a hot
midsummer night.

Dress you in west coast dreams,
and wake you up with
a Venice sunrise.

MEND

Let's mend our hearts
into origami stars and
light up a new sky just for us.

Let's read our palms
in the redwoods, study the
curvature of tides.

Let's fall in love
during a downpour
without irony.

FAST

I want to love you
in the fast lane, memorize
your laugh, and break
all the rules. I want you
to love me like it's going out of style.

Love me like it's
a secret you've
been dying to let out.

Love me like
fresh drops of rain
on your tongue.

Like you want to
devour me.

BLUE MOON

There's a blue moon
kind of love that
heals clipped wings
in one fell swoop.

SURPRISE ME
(for Griff)

It surprised me too.
I wasn't expecting it either.
So here we are. Each of us
daring the other to say yes first.

Surpirse me now.

I'm tired of guessing.
I want love to pour
from your mouth
like a waterfall

WEST

The wind pushes
me west, and sand
gets in my dreams.
I have overdue
meetings with life
in the desert.

I leave traces of
myself for you
to find me. Like
a fallen leaf in
wet cement.

ACT III

BIGGER THAN

I look at you,
and I see something
bigger than this life.

Some kind of energy
that has no home
but lives everywhere.

AT EASE

You put the wars in
my heart at ease.

I felt something bigger
than myself, a healing
instinct with enough
storms and sunlight
to flourish.

But I didn't know
what to do with
these extra bouncy
thoughts, I could
never catch.

Something was
rotten. Rotting.

So you uprooted
me. Showed me
my first super bloom.

Later, when I went
to look at the scars, I found
wild flowers in their place.
Look at this spectacular mess
we find ourselves in.

TOGETHER

We're lost together.
It's our kismet reunion.
A life of secrets in one glance.
Will you forgive the creak in our souls?

The way we draw our lines
on cliffs? When I'm with you,
I don't feel wrong
about who I am.

EASY HEAT

You give me that
easy heat, you're summer's
favorite song, and
when I see you,
my body can't help
but move towards yours.

You're the music of
my favorite love.

Our bodies already
know each other.
Now I know
what's always
been missing.

SHE LEFT

She left. The bath
still running. Swear words
soaked in sweat.

Others like her came by,
Their baths still running.
Their swear words
soaked in sweat.

Together, we made
waves, because we
wanted to wake up
to new horizons.

TONGUE

I can see the truth
dying to jump off
the tip of your tongue.

It's the scary part.
The part that
changes your story.

I can feel you thinking
about me. Just let it out
and let me in.

I KNOW

I know the ocean's alchemy,
because I live in a body
of restless waves.

&

I know all your
troubled waters,
because we come
from the same sea.

THE WORDS

I keep thinking about
the way you saw right
through me, and how
much I liked it.

I loved you for all
the words you
left on your tongue,
and all the looks you
gave me when people
spoke for too long
of nothing.

SORRY BUT

This is about the unfortunate
circumstances you find
yourself in presently.

Your head is a dirty room.

Filled with half empty cups
half-baked dreams, and
something is rotten.

I don't mean to go here. Recently
I've been made aware that I
come across as insensitive.

I don't want to go here
with you, but
I always do.

CALM DOWN

You threw your hands up.
You thought I was jealous,
because you were talking
to another woman that night.

I'm always talking to you, he said.
Even when I'm not talking to you,
I'm talking to you.

What is it you want now?
Forgiveness? A little inspiration?
And a slice of my light?

You're bored & now you want
The affection of a scorpio's sting,
but you'll change your mind.

You miss me as your muse. &
just can't seem to find another
that rises from the grave
quite like me.
I thought you knew that. Or else,
why would you bother
to begin with?

LIKE THIS

Tonight, I feel like
I could fall through the floor.
Evaporate to dust, but
you come home, and
show me where I hid
my laughter.

It's probably the nicest
gift anyone has ever
given. When someone
as funny and brilliant
as you, reminds me of
the humor in myself.

RIGHT THERE

You loved her at once.
Right there. And there.
And…there.And for
years you would love
her like that.

You would take her
outside of parties &
pour out your problems.
For what. For why.

You would bring cigarettes
and coffee in the early
morning as an offering
for more of her time.

But she could never
love you like that.
She loved you the way
she learned to love herself.

THAT MAN

He loved her because
he knew she could hold
the weight of his secrets.

He knew she wouldn't
put him on trial since
it was clear he
punished himself
by the haunting of his
lost heart. His confused
heart.

His heart fit on no map.
No trail laid with stones
for him to go down.

He is like me. A crow.
He is afraid of his history,
And doesn't trust his future.
He is jealous and careless
in the flash of a thought.

FAVORITE

Hearing my soul
after all these years
was like visiting
my favorite garden
I only ever see in dreams.

HAPPY

I'm happy to let you
go if it means holding
onto myself.

ASKING

Asking her to sight tight
is like asking the ocean
to sit still. Futile.

BACK THEN

Back then you wanted
me to chill.
But I wanted to
skinny-dip in
Lake Michigan.

Now I only want you.

I want to skinny dip
with only you in any
windfall of stars, and
bare our secrets to
the cosmos.

GET UP

I get up early to watch
the sunrise. The current
pulled me under for so many
times, twisted my body
in seaweed and sorrow
for so long, I wondered
if I would ever see
these colors again.

BETWEEN

I read between your waves,
and learn the secrets
of your blueprint.

I want to know
a life of joy like
I know the dead of night.

CRAVED

There were days
I craved ocean air
on my face, but
couldn't even get
out of bed.

When I should've
taken a hammer
to this frozen heart
instead of barely survivng.

There are still days when
I don't like anything
or anyone, including myself.

UNSEEN

I see the way your eye
catches the unseen, hides
it in a handkerchief, and
unveils a universe.

When I'm with you,
I don't feel wrong
about who I am.

It's hot when you're raw,
unedited, and swimming
in yourself.

WHAT I WANT

I feel the bass
in my body again.
Like the sun
of my heart
is all the way on,
like I'm gonna
do what I want.

Blackout.

About The Author

Grace Murphy lives in Los Angeles with her husband and their dog, Beckett. In 2019, she sold a story to Lifetime called, *Christmas Hotel*. *Surprise Me* is her first book, and she looks forward to sharing more.

Made in the USA
Coppell, TX
10 November 2020